Absence

Absence

Poems by

Nancy Manning

Cover design by Shay Culligan
Cover image by Nancy Manning
Author photo by Cori Patchkofsky

ISBN: 978-1-63980-993-6

Kelsay Books
502 South 1040 East, A-119
American Fork, Utah 84003
Kelsaybooks.com

to Beth and Larry

Acknowledgments

Thank you to the editors of *Connecticut Literary Anthology, Unmagnolia,* and *Sad Girl Diaries* for publishing my poems.

Thank you to my husband and our daughter for love and support and the Woodhouse family for so many years of friendship, to the late Harold Robinson for encouraging my creative writing during high school, to Jodie D'Alexander and Stephanie Amerigian for providing me with space to write.

Thank you for critiques from members of my writing groups: Laura, Ruth, Kathleen, Nancy, Karen, Elizabeth, and Bill.

Thank you to poet Nancy Naomi Carlson for reviewing my book and Vivian Shipley for suggestions in revising, ordering these poems, creating the title, and reviewing the book.

Contents

Give sorrow words. The grief that does not speak
Whispers the o'er-fraught heart, and bids it break.

—William Shakespeare

When I Return to My Neighborhood

Windsor Locks sleeps. But I remember livelier times.
Mike the milkman walking up our sidewalk as bottles clinked.
He tipped his hat, deposited our order in the metal bin, took the
    empties.

In front of Cobbs' house, the soda man parked his rusty van
that often backfired. Though I never saw him or what he delivered,
I always asked my mother why couldn't we drink soda?

The delivery man in sooty overalls dumped a load of coal outside
Gertie's cellar. Into her eighties, she'd shovel the black rocks
into a bin for her furnace. I'd hear the scrape of metal on cement.

Boys filled our backyard for a game of baseball. Batters
aimed for left field, strained to hit a ball at our cow barn,
shatter an unlucky window for us cheering fans.

We cluttered our den with summer bodies to watch
Dark Shadows. My brother repositioned rabbit ears to adjust
our failing TV. Without a fan, all us kids sweated, didn't mind.

In our clubhouse, we reenacted vampire and werewolf scenes.
Screamed when we were attacked. We hosted Halloween parties,
awarded prizes for the best costume, fastest bob for apple.

In winter we ice skated on Babiarz's pond. Blades glided
as we tried to figure skate graceful spins like Peggy Fleming.
Boys tore up the ice as they slammed a puck into a net of twigs.

We formed a kids' club. Held meetings by the chicken coop,
chanted a theme song—*Blackberry Hills, rah, rah, rah.*
Surrendered thumbs for pin pricks and blood promises.

We skipped to hopscotch in the driveway, shouted to Bob the
    Polish
man who walked by, returned home with a brown paper bag
under one arm. We rode bikes on a driveway course marked

by sheetrock chalk. Oftentimes, I raced up Sunset Street,
flew back down, my arms extended out like I was flying,
like I would be a kid forever, and death would never haunt me.

Noni's Cuckoo Clock

The gears would click and a little brown door
would open. A white bird would push
forward on his perch, nod, chirp once,

then disappear back into his home.
On the full hour, the bird would reappear,
chirp again. As early as three, I'd stand

under this treasure Noni brought back
from Italy. I'd watch, wait. Noni on the couch—
her nimble fingers knitting or crocheting—

she'd say *cuckoo* at odd moments and I would giggle.
Once I helped her pull the chains, set the hour.
Then time stopped. My heart broke losing her.

Noni and her knitted gifts were my world.
If only that clock were packed away somewhere,
I could reset the hour, hear that bird chime once more.

Six Days After My Mother Died

family handed me birthday cake with floral
swirls and fancy lettering.
                        But I felt sliced,
tossed the dessert into the trash.

On my calendar, I marked my mother's February
birthday with a heart, but I couldn't smile.

I watched March Madness games alone,
cheered for UConn though I wished she were
next to me,
                hypnotized by Geno's pacing.

Through the spring, a bluebird tapped
at my dining room window, chirped hello
as we played Five-Nine, Kings in the Corner,
Scrabble.
                I smiled, nodded at her.
In July and August, I started finding pennies—
heads up in parking lots. Tiny treasures
that appeared at my feet when I exited my car.
I closed my eyes, imagined they were notes
she tossed at my feet. *Liberty, In God we trust.*

During the pandemic, I hoped she heard me read
"Song of Myself" in my classroom.
Whitman's celebrating life, accepting death.
I tried to sound my own *barbaric yawp,*
but my shriek didn't make me feel better.

                                 During October
football games, I sat by myself. Kept my light off on Halloween.
Thanksgiving offered no crowd—only my husband, daughter,
as I picked at turkey, stuffing, gravy,
lemon meringue pie from her sacred recipe.

At Christmas I prayed to the baby Jesus
that he would lift my loneliness, offer an early spring.

Before Heading Off to College

I rescued my father's black and red check
jacket from the rag bag, packed in the corner
of the hallway closet.

My dad wore that woolen coat when I was a kid.
He'd head off on cold mornings for the first shift
at Dexter's papermill. Black lunchbox in hand,
he didn't kiss my mother's cheek or hug me good-bye
though he passed both of us at the kitchen table.
I watched him turn his back, open the back door,
head out. The still doorknob a final word.

Evenings when he returned, he'd hang
that jacket on a nail in the kitchen.

When I was five, I tried it on. The collar scratched
my cheeks; the sleeves itched my arms.

At eighteen, after my father had been dead a year,
I tried the coat on again. The flimsy fabric provided me
warmth and a faint smell of minty aftershave.

Without my mother watching, I replaced missing buttons.
Hand stitched red yarn in a zigzag pattern to repair a tear
in the shoulder. I cut up a black tee shirt to hide vast holes
that exposed my elbows.

My father would never see me graduate, walk
me up the aisle, or read a poem I'd written about him.
I needed that jacket.

November in Ariel Park

Inside the wrought iron fence, beyond the evergreens,
I pass row after row of headstones. Gray marble shapes
call out names in a dull monotone.
I locate his plot, kneel down, press my fingers
over the letters of his name, the numbers of his life.
He left too soon.
I exit the cemetery, visit the nearby playground.
No children swing, shoot down slides, charge in tag.
I lower myself on a swing. With my heel,
I scrape away dirt, peel away layers of skin. Feel
the tears. A figure approaches. I know the forward lean,
the slow steps, the blue eyes.
Maybe I have rubbed some lamp,
been granted this genie. I grip metal links of the swing.
He sits beside me, smiles.

He asks, *Why are you crying?* I sigh. Explain
that college makes me busy. My family is frozen in time.
Distance divides us. His feeble hand clasps mine.

He asks if I want tea. Daddy knew I don't drink coffee.
I shake my head, share summer stories of how I drove
my sister to cancer treatment, watched her suffer.

He says she will be fine and we will meet again.
I look up, he is gone. I squint, see no trace. I return
day after day, hopeful to see him, but he never reappears.

Where Crows Have Nowhere to Land

Bombs have gutted, reduced to rubble
building after building in Kyiv and beyond.

Ukraine is heaps of ash, recurring nightmare.

Streets are cluttered with corpses wild dogs can feed on.
Pools of blood stain the pavement.
                                    Behind trees
a few bodies stick out—partially buried in sand.
Only the lucky ones have been black bagged,
placed in mass graves, though unmarked.

Neighborhoods left empty by those who have fled
echo anguish.
                    We hear the elderly couldn't leave.
Groans of hunger, the need for water, heat.
Babushkas and blankets cannot keep out the cold.

Millions of refugees shuffle toward Poland—
most empty-handed.
                        Shock discolors their faces.

Loss after loss after loss. The present frazzles them.
The future a distant unknown.

Children board busses, touch window, meet the hand
of a father on the other side of glass.

                            No smiles
of farewell, no promise of a return home.

Postcard (Never Sent)

Children leap from the skeleton of a dock,
splash into the belly of this lake. Unable
to sleep, I watch from my window. My eyes
trace curves of mountains in this hazy afternoon.
I still hear the tapping of your tiny heart, still see
your image on the ultrasound—alive, vibrant.

Birdhouse

One little bluebird head peers out—
a circle the size of a quarter. The home
a wooden box on a metal foundation.
He waits for his mother's return.

She arrives with mealworms, later brings
more leaves and grass for their nest.
How this mother coddles her brood. One day
they will fly off. Leave home. And you

my darling daughter pack the car with clothes,
books, supplies—excited to head off
to college, use your able wings.

Your Absence

For years I'd hear the dull thud of morning
feet hitting the floor overhead. The hurried

steps across your room, your stomping
down the stairs. You'd grab a quick breakfast—

milkshake or crackers—then charge back upstairs,
slam the door. Water exploded in the shower.

Towels untidied the room, the floor puddled.
You'd head off to high school or work, a foot

heavy on the gas pedal down the driveway.

Now with you away at college, I straighten
the quilt on your bed, sit on the edge.

Silence disturbs my ears. My heart feels hollow.

I miss the tornado of your books, the volcano
of your clothes spewing forth from the closet

and drawers left open—the tidal wave of jewelry, powders,
papers, notebooks, oboe and guitars on your desk.

To make noise, I switch on the air purifier, imagine your return.

Our Own Walden

For eighteen years, every April, my daughter
and I have sojourned here at Lake Sunapee.

To breathe, read, reconnect. Snow has cleared,
ice disappeared. Buds dot the trees; crocuses

and daffodils welcome us back as chipmunks
race by. We enjoy the healing hands of this lake.

Each summer we return—to hike, glide
on a playground slide, challenge the other

at the Adventure Park, paddle kayaks, lounge,
absorb the sun. We dine on the dinner boat,

enjoy the tour. But this month, I travel alone.
Silence invades my trip. Kathleen left the nest

well before I wished her gone. A lone mallard
paddles to my dock, reminds me summer isn't far away.

Walking into History at the Susan B. Anthony Birthplace

My daughter and I start in the backroom
where shelving holds linen, bowls, cups, spoons.
We take steps that mirror the steps of pairs
of shoes attached to the ceiling of each room.

Little girl shoes—white and black—
with frilly lacing and straps. Little boy shoes—
brown, leather boots with rusted
eyelets and torn laces. Dozens of them
that had walked alongside their mothers,
aunts, grandmothers in parades,
demonstrations, pickets at the White House.

Into the kitchen apple pie bakes
in the oven. The cinnamon fragrance makes
our tongues water. To the front bedroom,
where Susan was born. Stacked in the corner,
blue blankets and quilts with swirl patterns.
A four-poster bed invites an afternoon nap.

Into the foyer, we pause. We can sneak a peek
upstairs or head out the front door or move
into the parlor to pose alongside Susan's cardboard
likeness. Short in her Victorian black, her eyeglasses
pinch her nose. Her face stern, determined
to right a wrong.

Onto the dining room, her timeline posted
of suffragist battles. We nod at the jail key token
commemorating her struggle. A reminder
never to give up, to protest an unfair law
and persevere to right its wrong.

Habibi (My Darling)

based on a CNN news report, December 2021

I watch the news and this story disrupts my soul.
An old man places two thousand afghani bills
in a father's hands, then grabs Pawana, the daughter.
She cowers, cries, pleads, drags her feet

on the clay road of this refugee camp.
Now able to feed his five other children,
the father keeps his head low—a life
sentence extended.

But what does a nine-year old know
of cooking, cleaning, serving a man?
Their oldest, just twelve, was sold off
only months ago while Pawana danced

in an open field. Her pink dress emblazoned
against a brown background that contrasted
with her ruddy cheeks. A blue hijab highlighted
her eyes, covered her curls.

If only their darling Pawana could be returned.
She'd be schooled, dream big like my daughter, maybe
even become a teacher like me. Not have
her wishes collected, discarded like trash.

Myrtle

Devil in my flower bed,
you creep across my mulch, sink
claws deep into compost, and stretch

your limbs to reach my irises.
You squeeze leafy fingers to choke their stems.
You wink at my lilies, send more vines to strangle.

You render four o'clocks, marigolds,
roses defenseless too. Your purple petals blow
cold kisses at my pachysandra. Your breathy whispers

smother my dianthus. I can almost hear
you sneer. You tempt me with your beauty. I want
to make a crown of your laurel. But I resist,

eradicate the jungle of you, free flowers despite
the aching of my back and hands. Dump you
in the refuse pile to rot.

Four High School Girls

In her dented blue Chevy, Beth drove us
to Lake Sunapee, back in August '81.
We chatted about colleges, confessed crushes,
mimicked the voice of our chemistry teacher.

We stayed at Buringtons' cottage, painted
green and gold, hidden amongst pines
in the harbor—a wrap-around porch,
seater swing and collection of stoves

bought at tag sales and lugged here.
Inside the cabin, a post and beam ceiling,
soft chairs that didn't cushion our backs.
A kitchen in need of scrubbing. Family photos

plastered the walls. Magazines scattered about.
A rickety loft. We sunned at Dewey Beach,
dipped our toes in water glimmering under the dock,
even water skied. Feasted on waffles at the Woodbine.

Enjoyed lunch, dinner, ice cream at The Anchorage.
Spent days searching for Steven Tyler and nights
listening to bands at the gazebo. We closed our eyes.
Dreamed of running a B-and-B here.

Never leaving. The four of us a team.
But after college, we broke apart. Ann stayed
in South Bend; Maria moved to Colorado.
Each of us married, became mothers.

Beth and I returned to Sunapee many times.
After she died, I walked the harbor alone. Sat outside
the Wild Goose. Boarded the dinner cruise myself.
Watched the moon glow, her smile on this earth's eye.

Two High School Friends

In April of that year, Beth and I strolled
        through Elizabeth Park, smiled
at the stories we shared with each other.
        The roses hadn't woken up yet.

Rows and rows of red and pink, buds
        waiting to burst forth from vines
tightly woven around arches
        we passed through. They listened.

They must have. We promised
        to return in June. But never did.
Then you died on Christmas Eve.

        Now I tend my own rose plants.
Trim the jagged shoots that lean
        into the azalea, disturb irises, overpower
four o'clocks.

I sprinkle ashes, water and spray them.
        Sweet fragrances fill the summer air.
I place a bouquet by your grave
        though thorns scratch my skin.

Finding Beth

My husband and I fight wind, slog our feet
toward the cell tower. In snow and slush,
halfway up our shins, we ignore soggy
sneakers and socks as we cut across graves,

mar them with footprints. Before us, hedges
separate this cemetery from a baseball field.
Behind us, Plank Hill Road. At the Marum marker,
we pause. The headstone a granite gray in the shape

of a bench, so all can rest, reminisce about Bob.
And below that bench, another granite marker
with a Celtic cross and a musical note. Your name
ornately inscribed: *Beloved wife.* Birth date, death

date. But time hasn't healed my wound, lightened
my heart—cleared away clouds.

Tug-of-War

Ours was a bond of pulling.
You attracting with

sapphire eyes, a shy
smile. Me extracting your thoughts—

longing to call you more than Beth's brother,
wanting to understand

why darkness plagued you, Larry.
You signed a letter "Fondly," sang

me "Golden Slumbers." I found
your heart tender,

repositioned footing.
Dreamt we'd clasp hands,

hungered to feel your lips find mine.
I tightened my grip

as I strained,
pulled harder, harder.

Hands blistered with blood.
The rope began to fray.

I let go. You fell back,
looked away. Your pulse difficult

to track. News of your suicide strangled
like a cord around my neck.

If we were given one day, I'd hold on
longer, bleed from wounds even deeper.

At Hammonasset Beach

Wind whips my face this March morning. Clouds
discolor the sky. Sand stretches for miles east,

west—footprinted, littered, though empty of guests.
Years ago that July, lovers held hands, ran into

the embrace of Long Island Sound, kissed.
Children sifted sand, filled buckets, built castles.

Teenagers threw Frisbees, blasted radios, feasted on
sandwiches, foil wrapped. How the ocean lured us

with words. *Let my cool waters soothe you.*
I stood, dove in, didn't leave till sunset. A friend

several blankets away, also left, both of us too shy
to say hello as waves washed away our steps.

Today the distant sun reminds me summer is months
away, and you are on another shore, a world away.

At St. Mary's Cemetery

This poinsettia I place
alongside your headstone on Christmas Day—
yellow cyathia diamonds explode like your smile.
Vibrant cultivars and leaves complete the red,
green holiday scheme.

I feel sun
warm my face as on our many hikes
through forest, off main trails.

I return on New Year's Day.
Fight bitter wind. Hear snow crunch under my boots.
I find brown leaves shriveled in thirsty soil
like the collapse of your life. I kneel, breathe.
Search my mind for happier times.

How you sacrificed
for football—your body bruised and bleeding.
I cheered you, star of my Bethlehem.

On Deaf Ears

From the west shore of Fernwood Point,
I see the moon. A one-eyed goddess
that glares, never blinks.

The curve of her lens forms
a gray circle, almost full.
She bewitches,

pressures my confession.
I pierced a high school heart,
later broke it. Blue-eyed, bearded

in flannel shirt and jeans,
he loved hiking. Died before
I could apologize.

Tonight, I want to reverse time.
But my prayers fail.
I feel no atonement.

Only more guilt.
Maybe a gentler moon watches
over him, forgives.

Henry

Through the spring, I wheeled him to the park.
We fed ducks pieces of bread, watched them
step into patient water, which spread in circles
then fizzled away.

This gray man—the grandpa I never had—
told me stories about his farm, decades before
I started working there. As a boy, he milked cows,
peddled free range eggs, strawberries.

He drove the tractor before he was a teen.
In straight rows he cut hay, kicked it, bundled it.
Loaded bales himself in back breaking work,
delighted when summer rain

tickled his face, cooled him off.
                                One day when I
was working the produce stand, he paused, pointed
to double rainbows beaming in the sky, offered
them both to me with a wink.

I wasn't in the convalescent home when he gasped
his last breath.
                Nurses said
                he had been smiling.

When his casket rested by his headstone,
pairs of eyes glared, his family stared with eager lips.

Before sunset, they emptied his farmhouse, filled
their arms with copper, tin, glass, his rocking chair
with cane seat. I adorned his grave with geraniums.
Let raindrops nourish their petals.

Against the Current

From my student's hawk-like talons hangs
a dangling mouse that squirms to free

herself before he threatens to drop her
remains.
           Day after day, she begs him

to stop keeping an eye trained on her every
high school step. Stop blackening her eyes.

Stop dashing her dreams to the ground.
If only she could escape the stretch of his wingspan,

heal her wounds.
           If only there were music,
of minds floating together. Instead I fear

a future of final breaths, a Pollack canvas
of splattered blood and flesh from a devouring.

seaside

morning whispers
from balcony
into room.

curtain swells
white like a ghost.
our bodies still
on sheets

until you leave
my arms.

heart pulls away from
heart,
legs loosen—
splitting us in half

i lower my head
like the rose
that surrenders
too early
a secret

Tattooed

For four years, I have watched this pair.
Despite his injury, JD can still block, tackle
on the gridiron, never fails to get up.
The announcer repeats "D'Angelo"
for defensive stands to our cheering fans.

On the court, Robby pounds the boards—
feet in position, arms extended. The quick
release of a three-pointer in the corner.
An easy two in the paint. A towering block.
Our crowd drowns out the play-by-play.

The two sit in my classroom, in the front.
They waste little time, complete their work,
never complain. Their politeness pleases me.

Both honor their mothers.
On JD's left arm, a red rose inside
a black wooden cross. "Dawn" and the dates
of her birth and death. A heavenly blue background.

On Rob's left arm, "Mom" in the center.
A cross above and below the name.
Gray clouds in a celestial background.

Through discipline and faith, these Woodland
seniors have tattooed my heart. Graduation
a date in June not far away, their names
enshrined in gold ink, "Hawks."

Bond Unbroken

to my student Lori Jackson Gellatly (1981–2014)

I study it daily. Run my fingertips
over the tightly knit surface.
My daughter—her brunette hair
tied back, her brown eyes focused—
wove its thin strands,

wrapped it around my wrist,
knotted it. A chevron pattern
of red, white, blue, purple—
my favorite colors. Someday
it will fray, split apart, but we won't.

A mother's bond to her daughter
never breaks.

Mrs. Jackson told the court
these words, the day her son-in-law
was sentenced for murdering Lori.

That May 7th morning, Scott broke
into the kitchen, shot the dog,
fired a bullet at Mrs. Jackson. Lori yelled,
"Don't hurt Mommy," intercepted more bullets.

No restraining order could stop Scott.
The police arrived too late, found
the bloodbath. A bullet fired
into Mrs. Jackson's arm, another entered her brain,
blinded one eye. Her pulse a faint whisper.

Lori, shot in the heart, remained lifeless.
A condition no medical staff could reverse.

Devil's Arrow

This dragonfly has targeted me all week.
Buzzed around my dock at Chalk Pond,

edged closer not to pierce but tickle my feet,
use my arm as a runway. He's given me time

to scrutinize the velvety black of his eyes,
thorax, segmented abdomen. Such symmetry—

two pairs of legs, two pairs of wings, translucent
with a mosaic of lines and dark markings

on the upper tips. Maybe jealousy tortured
his human soul. I name him Heathcliff

though in his insect life, he doesn't seem haunted.
There's no sting or bite. Only carefree flight.

In my mind, I'm his Catherine. I fly away with him.
Together we escape the earthly load of life.

During These Troubled Times

they still smile at us—
this garden, this congregation of irises Van Gogh

captured in oils. Friendly features deep blue, thoughtful.
Orange hearts in the center. Striations lively with lines.

Their green stems lean toward the sun.
Thick like vines, yellow inlays support these blossoms

and buds not yet open.
                        How they dazzle,
absorb the light, hum in unison.

Soil rusty brown, fertile with life.
                        They stretch
clusters of rhizomes above ground
so they can multiply, multiply, multiply.

A softer blue flower off to the right sings his lyrics.
Words this chorus echoes.

And one single white blossom to the left
stands out. Is alive, not lonely.
                        Voice graceful,
she defies being picked or forgotten.

At Snow Lake in Summer

From a park bench, I watch
this trio of Canada geese,
this family.

Their bodies float—brown
feathers, black heads, white-
ringed necks,

dark eyes. Webbed feet propel
them around the cluster
of water lilies.

Spotting me, they perform—
swim in straight lines. Then
perfect circles.

They bow heads when finished.
The young one decides
to explore on her own,

taps her mother's beak goodbye.
What can the mother do but watch
her swim away?

About the Author

Nancy Manning lives in Connecticut and teaches high school English classes. She holds an MFA in Poetry from Southern Connecticut State University.

Her poems appear in numerous publications, most recently *Connecticut Literary Anthology, Humans of the World, Sad Girl Diaries, Noctua Review,* and *Unmagnolia.* Her poetry collections are *Amethyst Garden* (Jasmin Press, 2002), *The Unspoken of Our Days* (Antrim House, 2022), and *What Glues Us Together* (Antrim House, 2023); her novel *Undertow of Silence* (TAG Publishing, 2013) won the TAG Publishing award for Best New YA novel.